Contents

Homes 4

Tent House 6

Houseboat.................................. 8

Raft House................................ 10

Stilt House 12

Tree House 14

Sky Home 16

On Wheels 18

Holiday House........................ 20

Glossary 22

Further Reading 23

Index 24

KT-362-471

Homes

Most people live in homes that do not move. They live in houses or flats that stay still.

Moving houses

Some people need to live in houses that can move. They take the houses with them as they travel.

When most people move, they do not move their house with them!

Air, land, water

Some people live in very wet places. They need houses that can move on water, or sway in trees high up above the water below.

Moving house

Tent House

Nomads are people who live in tents, which they carry with them wherever they go.

Follow the animals

Nomads keep animals such as camels and goats. When the animals move to find food, the nomads go with them.

*Many nomads live in hot **deserts**.*

Hot and cold

Some nomads live in hot places where there are deserts. Others live in grassy places where it can be cold.

Let's go!

Houseboat

A houseboat is a boat that people live on. It has rooms for sleeping and for cooking.

All year round

Some people live on houseboats all the time. They tie up their boat on the **waterway**, or in a **harbour**.

Chug, chug!

Just holidays

Some houseboats are used just for holidays. People use them to travel slowly along rivers, lakes, or **canals**.

Many houseboats are painted bright colours.

Raft House

Some people live in floating homes. There are even floating villages! They move from side to side in the water.

All aboard

A floating village has no roads and no cars or trucks. Everything is brought to the village by boat.

*Floating villages are built on **rafts**.*

Fish food

The people in this floating village catch fish. They sell some of the fish to people on the land.

Keep paddling!

Stilt House

Houses built beside rivers or the sea are easily flooded. **So some people build their houses on** stilts.

Up and down

Some stilt houses have metal stilts. The houses slide up and down the stilts. When the water rises, the houses move up the stilts.

High and dry

Strong stilts

The stilts on houses are so strong that they do not move in the flowing water. The house on top stays still and dry.

These stilt houses are made of wood.

13

Tree House

How would you like to live at the top of a tree? Some people build their houses there.

No water up here!

The Korowai people live in **swamps** that often flood, so they build their houses high up in the trees. The houses sway in the wind with the trees.

It's a long climb to the front door!

Tree trip

Some **wildlife parks** have tree houses. Visitors can sleep safely in the trees, away from wild animals below.

Don't look down!

15

Sky Home

Homes at the top of skyscrapers **are higher above the ground than any other home.**

Are we moving?
A skyscraper is built to sway in strong winds, although people may not feel it moving.

Sky high!

16

Don't move!

Very tall buildings are sometimes built with heavy water tanks on top. This stops the buildings from moving too much.

You get a bird's eye view from the top of a skyscraper.

On Wheels

Caravans and camper vans **are homes that people can drive from place to place.**

Pull or drive?

Camper vans have an engine, so they can be driven. Caravans do not have engines, so must be pulled by a car.

On the road

Gypsy caravans are often painted with bright colours.

Gypsy house

Gypsies and travellers live in caravans all year round. They used to travel in their caravan from place to place, but today they usually stay in a special campsite.

Holiday House

Have you ever slept in a tent?
Lots of people live in a tent
when they go on holiday.

Home in a minute

You can take a tent anywhere
you are allowed to camp. Most
tents fit over a metal frame
and are easy to put up.

Holiday time

Sleep and eat

Campers usually cook food on a barbeque or on a small **gas stove**. They zip themselves into a sleeping bag at night.

Camping can be a lot of fun.

Glossary

camper vans vans you can live in

canals waterways that boats travel on

deserts dusty, dry, and rocky places

flooded covered with water

gas stove small cooker powered by gas

gypsies people who travel and live in caravans

harbour area by the sea where boats are kept

nomads people who travel with their animals

rafts lengths of wood tied together

skyscrapers tallest type of buildings

stilts tall poles that hold up a house on top

swamps watery places with very soggy ground

waterway river or canal boats travel along such as a river or canal

wildlife parks places people can visit to see animals in the wild

Further Reading

Websites

See more photographs of stilt houses at:
www.visualgeography.com/categories/thailand/houses

Look at some great tree house pictures at:
www.weburbanist.com/2008/02/10/10-amazing-tree-houses-from-around-the-world-sustainable-unique-and-creative-designs/

Click on Homes to find different games about houses at:
www.bbc.co.uk/schools/websites/4_11/site/geography

Books

Homes (Starters) by Rosie McCormick, Wayland (2005).

Homes on the Move (Homes Around the World) by Nicola Barber, Wayland (2007).

Index

animals 6, 15

boats 8–9, 10

camper vans 18–19
canals 9
caravans 18–19
cooking 8, 20

deserts 6, 7

fish 11
floating villages 10–11
flooded 12, 14

gas stove 20
gypsies 19

harbour 8
holidays 9, 20–21
houseboats 8–9

Korowai 14

nomads 6–7

rafts 10–11

skyscrapers 16–17
stilts 12–13
swamps 14

tents 6, 20
tree houses 14–15

water 5, 8–9, 10–11, 12–13
waterway 8
wildlife parks 15
winds 16

24